FROM DIAGNOSIS TO SURVIVAL

Then, Now, and Beyond — A Journey of
Faith, Humor, and Healing

____

By Marlita (Marli) Blackman

From Diagnosis to Survival
Copyright © 2022 by **Marli Blackman**

ISBN: **979-8-218-87009-6**

Order: www.marliblackman.com

DEDICATION

For my son, Frank Jermaine Blackman Jr.

You are the best human I know.

You made motherhood a piece of cake — full of laughter, purpose, and unconditional love.

Your strength carried me through my hardest days, your humor lifted me when I felt weak,

And your heart reminded me that I had every reason to keep fighting.

And to my bonus baby, Arrington R. Blackman (RIP) —

Thank you for taking care of your little brother while your little brother checked on me. Your spirit still fills every room, every thought, and every quiet moment.

You are my eternal light — proof that love never leaves, it just transforms.

This book is for both of you — for the bond that even time and heaven can't break, and for every mother who knows that her children are her heartbeat and her healing.

TABLE OF CONTENTS

FOREWORD

I've known Marli Blackman for more than fifteen years — long enough to see her in every light: the professional, the friend, the mother, the fighter, the woman of faith. We've done business together from Kansas to Chicago and just about everywhere in between. No matter the city or the setting, she has always been the same woman — grounded, focused, and driven by purpose.

Her mind is her superpower. Her faith is her foundation. And her perseverance is the thread that runs through everything she touches.

When Marli walks into a room, the atmosphere shifts. She doesn't need to demand attention — she earns it. She leads with grace, commands with quiet confidence, and treats everyone with kindness and respect. She gives more than most people even think to offer.

Through every challenge, Marli has shown a strength that humbles you. Life has tested her in ways that would've broken many, but she never wavered. She fought back with faith, humor, and an unshakable sense of self — and this book, From Diagnosis to Survival, is living proof of that fight.

What you're holding isn't just a story about survival. It's a testimony to what happens when faith meets fire and purpose refuses to quit. Every page carries her honesty, her wit, and her light. She invites you in — not as a victim of circumstance, but as a victor who turned pain into purpose and loss into legacy.

If you know Marli, you know she loves deeply, gives freely, and stands firmly in truth. The world is lucky to have her — though some days, I still don't think we deserve her.

So take your time with this book. Read it when you need courage. Revisit it when you need joy. And remember, just like Marli shows us here: survival isn't the end of the story — it's the beginning of something far more powerful. Marli — thank you for showing us what strength, faith, and love look like in motion. We love you.

    — Hawaii

PREFACE

There are moments that split life into before and after. The day I got my diagnosis was one. Everything slowed, sounds faded, and all I could hear was my heartbeat, trying to process the words. Nothing would be the same—yet I sensed this wasn't the end. The journey that followed taught me more about faith, strength, and grace than I ever expected. Some days I cried, some nights I prayed, and some mornings I laughed just to prove I was still here. I learned survival isn't about what happens to you—it's about what happens through you.

This book was born from those moments—the quiet, chaos, and courage it took to stand again. It's about more than a diagnosis. It's every storm, every setback that became a setup, and each time God whispered, "Get up, you still have work to do." I didn't want just a story. I wanted a companion and light for anyone facing diagnosis, heartbreak, or detours. Here are my truths, and also laughter, games, recipes, and bits of joy. Healing isn't always heavy; sometimes, it's a crossword or dancing in your kitchen, or reliving the memories that remind you of your purpose.

This book is for survivors—of illness, loss, fear, or anything that tried to break you. It's for anyone who's thought, "I don't know how I'll make it," and somehow did.

If you take nothing else, know this: you are still here for a reason.

That reason is bigger, brighter, and more beautiful than you can imagine.

— Marli Blackman

INTRODUCTION

There are two clocks in a survivor's life: the one that measures minutes, and the one that measures meaning. After my diagnosis, I started paying attention to both. Some days moved slowly—drips, scans, questions, prayers. Others moved fast—the sound of my son's laughter in the kitchen, the way sunlight hit the table, the miracle of waking up to another morning. This book was born in the space between the two.

You will not find a perfect story here. You will find a true one. The truth is that I was afraid and faithful, determined and exhausted, laughing and crying—often in the same hour. I wrote these pages to make room for the whole experience of survival: the science and the spirit, the facts and the feelings, the medicine and the music. I also wrote them because somewhere, a mother is whispering to herself, "How do I tell my child I'm sick?" Somewhere, a son is peaking in a doorway to make sure his mom is still breathing. Somewhere, someone is sitting in a parking lot, gathering the courage to walk into another appointment. If that's you, this book is a hand on your back saying, "Keep going."

This is not a book about illness; it's a book about life. Cancer was the storm that rearranged the furniture, but the story is about what stayed: my faith, my son, my laughter, my purpose. I learned that survival is a team sport and a daily decision. It is the power to say, "This diagnosis is not the author of my life—I am." It is also the grace to admit, "I can be strong and still need help."

You'll see that reflected in the shape of these chapters:

- **"The Diagnosis"** is the doorway. It's the moment time split, the night I told my son, and the sentence that changed our schedule but not our destiny.

- **"The Battle Begins"** is the valley and the climb. It's about the rituals that kept me feeling like myself, the days' courage looked like soup and a spoon, and the quiet ways God sent help.

- **"My Survival Toolkit"** is exactly what it sounds like— faith, boundaries, nourishment, movement, humor, and gratitude. It's a set of practices you can pick up and personalize.

- **"Now—Living in the Moment"** explores the strange stillness after the chaos, the way the world stopped with COVID-19 just as my body needed stillness, and how peace can be learned on purpose.

- **"Beyond—A Life Reimagined"** is the invitation to thrive. It's about significance over speed, legacy over labels, and the new definitions of beauty, success, and joy that emerged after the fire.

You'll also find sections that are lighter by design: a feel-good watchlist for when you need a laugh, a word search for the days your mind needs gentle focus, and journal prompts for when your heart needs a place to land. Healing can be heavy. I wanted this book to breathe with you—to balance the weight with relief, the tears with giggles, the fight with rest.

A note about voice: you'll hear God all through these pages. My faith is not a plot device; it's the plot. That said, you don't have to believe what I believe to find yourself here. You only have to believe in a tomorrow you cannot yet see. Call it God, grace, grit, or simply the next right step—hope is welcome by any name.

A note about care: I am not prescribing a path; I am describing mine. You'll read about medical treatment, holistic support, and lifestyle changes I made with guidance. None of this replaces your doctor. Let it inspire questions, not shortcuts. Let it remind you that advocacy is love—that asking, learning, researching, and deciding are part of how you care for yourself.

A note about love: motherhood is the drumbeat under every page. My son, Frank Jr., is my reason and my rhythm. My bonus baby, Arrington (RIP), is my light in every room. If you've ever loved someone so much that you learned new levels of strength just to make them breakfast—then you already understand this book.

How to use this book?

- **Start anywhere.** If today calls for courage, begin with Chapter Two. If you need tools, jump to Chapter Three. If you want to remember joy, find the watchlist or the journal prompts.

- **Write in it.** Circle lines. Add dates. Tuck in test results and answered prayers. Let these pages become proof of your progress.

- **Share it.** Read a paragraph to a friend who doesn't know what to say. Leave it open where your child can see you turning the page. Hope is contagious; pass it on.

- **Rest with it.** On days when all you can do is breathe and believe, let this book sit beside you like a quiet companion. Healing counts even when it looks like stillness.

If you only remember one thing, let it be this: you are not your diagnosis; you are your divine comeback. You are allowed to be messy and magnificent, scared and brave, weepy and wise. There is room for all of you here. There is room for all of you in your own life.

So, inhale. Unclench your jaw. Loosen your shoulders. Take the next step—even if it's just turning the page.

Welcome.

CHAPTER ONE

There are some moments in life you can never prepare for —
moments that split your world into before and after. The day I got
my diagnosis was one of those moments, marking a clear line
between everything I knew before and everything that would
come after.

I remember sitting in Dr. Amanda Yancy's office — my dear
friend, my OB-GYN — when she said the words no one ever
wants to hear:

"You have cancer."

Everything that came after those three words disappeared into
a blur. The air changed. The room felt smaller. I could hear her
voice, but I couldn't process the meaning. It was as if I was
underwater — her words echoing and fading, like I was there but
not really there.

I stared at her lips moving, trying to focus on the words, but
my mind had already left the room.

Cancer? Me? How?

I had always taken care of myself — eaten right, prayed often,
worked hard, kept my faith strong. How could this be happening
to me?

I felt my hands gripping the edge of the chair, holding on as if
the world was tilting. My heart raced, my breath shortened, and
everything I thought I understood about life — about my life —
began to shift.

All I could think about was my son. My baby. My reason.

What would happen to him if I didn't make it?

Who would check on him the way I did, love him the way I
do, remind him every morning that he could conquer the world?

The thought of leaving him behind crushed me more than the diagnosis itself.

When I got home, the house was quiet — but my mind was loud. The kind of loud that shakes your spirit. Fear, confusion, disbelief — they all came rushing in at once. As the reality of the doctor's office faded, I sat in the dark for a while, just listening to the sound of my own heartbeat.

Later that night, once I'd gathered my thoughts, I called my son into the living room. He was only sixteen — still a boy in some ways, but with a soul wise beyond his years. I looked him in his eyes and said softly, "Baby, I have cancer."

He didn't flinch or cry. He looked at me with determination and said, "Mom, we'll get through this."

That's it. No hesitation. No doubt. Just certainty.

That moment changed everything. Because in his eyes, I saw faith — not fear. Strength — not pity. And I knew right then that if he believed we could make it, then I had no choice but to believe it too.

My son has always been the strongest man I know — even when he was just sixteen. That's how old he was when he thought he might lose me, and I thought I might lose everything. But his faith anchored me. His confidence in me made me remember who I was before fear showed up.

After he went to bed, I stood in front of the mirror and barely recognized the woman staring back. I saw the fear in my eyes — but I also saw the fight. The spirit. The refusal to quit.

And that's when it happened. I looked myself dead in the eye and said out loud, "F*** this. F*** cancer. Let go. I have to get back to my life."

It wasn't a whisper. It was a declaration. A promise. A prayer.

In that moment, something shifted inside me. I started to breathe again. I started to feel the life in my body again. I started to believe that healing wasn't just possible — it was already on its way.

That was the first day of my fight. Not the day I was diagnosed — but the day I decided that diagnosis didn't define me.

From that moment forward, I wasn't a patient — I was a warrior.

I wasn't going to let cancer write my story.

I was going to write it myself — with faith, fire, and a whole lot of fight.

CHAPTER TWO

When my son would ask, "Mom, are you okay?" I'd smile through it all and say, "Absolutely, baby."

I said it so many times it almost became a script — one that hid the truth of how I really felt. Because the truth? Some days I wasn't okay. Some days, the weight of it all felt like too much.

But I was determined that my son would never see me give up. Not once.

He had already seen enough — the hospital visits, the doctors' calls, the tears I tried to hide behind closed doors. I didn't want him to see fear in my eyes. I wanted him to see a fight.

So, I put on my armor every day — not made of metal, but of makeup, faith, and mental strength.

I'd wake up, brush my hair—what was left—then remind myself, you still got it, girl. I'd get dressed, even just to move from bed to couch. As long as I was moving, I was winning.

And that's the thing about this battle — it's more mental than physical. The body fights hard, but the mind has to fight harder.

At first, I tried to act like nothing had changed. I wanted to keep life as normal as possible. I'd still cook when friends came by, even when I had no energy. It wasn't about the food — it was about control. If I could stand in my kitchen and season a pan of chicken, then cancer hadn't taken everything.

They'd say, "Marli, sit down. Rest."

And I'd say, "No, because if I sit down, I might not get back up."

I wasn't trying to be a hero. I was trying to stay myself.

Cancer wanted to steal my strength, my style, my joy — all the things that made me who I am. And I refused to give it that satisfaction.

Some days, I woke up ready for anything—then exhaustion and pain hit. My body said, "You're not in charge," and I'd answer, "Oh yes, I am."

And then came the part no one really talks about — losing your hair.

I'll be honest: I despised wigs. Lace fronts styles — no judgment to anyone who wears them — they just weren't for me. I couldn't do it. Quiet as kept, I wore my hair really short—a pageboy cut—before I was even diagnosed. So, when my hair started to fall out, it wasn't about losing vanity; it was about losing part of my identity.

I rarely went anywhere. I didn't want to. But if I had to go somewhere, I'd throw on the wig just to get through it. Smile, show up, handle business, and then come home and rip that thing off the minute I close the door.

It's painful writing this, even now — five years later. I can hardly see the screen in real time because my eyes fill with water with every keystroke. These memories, they don't fade. They live under your skin, even after you've healed. But this is part of the truth — and truth is what set me free.

At that time, I was the Press Secretary for the City of Highland Park — a small city within a city — and I also hosted a local political TV show for the city. I loved that job. I loved using my voice, connecting with people, and bringing the community together. But after the diagnosis, I didn't feel like myself anymore. I didn't feel beautiful, confident, or strong. I didn't feel Marli.

So, I canceled the show. I told myself it was temporary, but really, it was because I didn't recognize the woman in the mirror. My smile felt forced, my light dimmed. During that pause, I struggled to regain my sense of purpose.

Then one day, just as I was questioning my next steps, the mayor called me and said, "Marli, I need you to interview someone important. It's just one show."

I hesitated. I didn't want to. But something in me said Go. So, I agreed.

That decision changed my life.

When I walked into the studio that day, my producer — who had worked with me for years — looked at me and said nothing at first. He just studied me for a moment. Later, when we were alone, he finally asked, "Where have you been?"

I hesitated again, but I told him the truth: "I've been sick."

He nodded quietly, then leaned closer and said, "Marli, I know someone. A holistic doctor. I think you should talk to him."

That conversation — in that little studio — was the beginning of my healing journey.

He introduced me to a holistic practitioner who changed everything. This man put me on a regimen that I still thank God for to this day: silver water, iodine, mineral greens, a liquid complex multivitamin, and a few other supplements. He helped me shift my diet completely — clean foods, no toxins, no junk, no processed anything. It wasn't easy, but I trusted the process.

And then, something miraculous happened.

I watched the tumor begin to dissipate.

I remember looking at the scans and the progress and just crying. Not because I was sad, but because I knew that what I was doing — this balance of faith, medical treatment, and holistic care — was working. God had aligned me with the right people at the right time.

That's when I truly began to believe that healing isn't onesize-fits-all. It's not just pills or chemo or supplements — it's faith, energy, intention, and obedience. It's learning to listen to your body when it whispers before it has to scream.

There's no manual for this kind of fight. Some mornings I'd wake up mad at the world. Some nights I'd wake up crying. But no matter what, every single day, I chose to live.

Because I realized something early on: cancer can touch your body, but it can't touch your soul.

It can shave your head, but it can't take your crown.

It can slow your walk, but it can't stop your purpose.

And it can try to silence you, but I promise — I was not about to go quietly.

I remember one day during treatment, I looked around the room at other patients. Some were reading, some were sleeping, some just staring into space — all of us in different parts of the same battle. I caught the eye of one woman who looked terrified, tears streaming down her face.

And something in me said, "Talk to her."

I leaned over and said, "You're stronger than you think, baby. You're already fighting. You're already winning just by being here."

She smiled through her tears. And that's when I realized — this journey wasn't just about me surviving. It was about helping others survive, too.

When I was home, my son became my shadow. He'd peek into my room every hour. "Mom, you need anything?"

"No, baby. I'm good."

"Are you sure?"

"I'm sure."

He'd nod and leave, but I could hear him in the hallway pacing, listening, making sure I was still breathing.

He was sixteen going on forty. My protector, my caretaker, my peace.

And I knew that even though he was scared, he never showed it. He learned to be strong because he saw me being strong. We were feeding off each other's faith.

One night, when I was too weak to eat, he sat on the edge of my bed with a bowl of soup he'd warmed up himself. "Come on, Mom," he said, "just a few bites."

I didn't want to. I felt like my body didn't belong to me anymore. But the way he looked at me — with love, with patience — I picked up that spoon.

That's when I realized — healing isn't just physical. It's spiritual. It's emotional. It's a team effort.

And our team was small, but mighty.

There were moments when friends would come by with flowers, food, or just laughter. And I needed that laughter more than any medicine. We'd talk trash, watch comedies, tell stories — and for a few hours, I'd forget I was sick.

Then there were nights when it was just me and God. I'd lie there in silence, staring at the ceiling, saying, "Lord, I don't know how to do this. But I know you do."

And every single time, I'd feel His peace settle over me like a warm blanket. That's what faith does — it steps in when strength runs out.

It wasn't a perfect fight. There were setbacks, scares, bad test results, and moments when the "what ifs" screamed louder than my prayers. But I refused to let fear win.

I told myself, "Marli, this is not the end. This is a reroute. God's just changing the scenery, not the destination."

So, I kept going. I kept showing up — to appointments, to life. Because every day I woke up was proof that I was still in the game. And one thing about me?

I don't quit mid-game.

CHAPTER THREE

When you're fighting for your life, you start realizing what really matters — what gives you strength, what drains it, and what you absolutely refuse to live without.

I didn't learn that in a hospital or a doctor's office. I learned it in my kitchen, in quiet mornings, in my prayer closet, and in those small moments when I could've fallen apart but chose not to.

I didn't want to just survive — I wanted to live.

So, I built what I call my Survival Toolkit — the things that helped me get my spirit, body, and peace back in alignment. Not everything in this toolkit can be found in a store or a prescription. Some of it came from prayer, some from stubbornness, and some from love.

Faith — My First Line of Defense

My first and strongest weapon was — and will always be — my faith.

I talked to God as if He were sitting right next to me. Some days, my prayers were soft whispers. Other days, they were full-on conversations that probably made my neighbors wonder who I was talking to.

I didn't wait until I "felt strong" to pray. I prayed when I was angry, when I was grateful, and when I didn't even have words. And every single time, I felt a little lighter.

There's something powerful about surrender — not giving up but handing it over. Saying, "God, this is too heavy for me. You carry it now." That's what kept me sane when fear tried to creep back in.

Faith became my medicine, my counselor, my calm.

The Mental Game — Cancer Was Not the Boss of Me

I decided early on that cancer wasn't going to control my mind. My body could be tired, but my spirit untouchable.

I created routines that made me feel normal — even when nothing about life felt normal. I got up, showered, and dressed every single day, even if all I did was move from my bed to the couch. I'd look in the mirror and say, "You still got it, girl."

And I meant it.

When people called with fear in their voices, I quickly shut it down. I couldn't afford to let pity into my atmosphere. I told them, "If you're not calling to make me laugh, pray, or bring joy — don't call."

Protecting my peace was part of my healing plan. I learned that energy is medicine, too.

Cancer might have been in my body, but it was not going to take over my mind. That was my promise to myself.

Laughter — My Secret Superpower

Comedy saved my sanity.

When I couldn't find strength in my body, I found it in laughter. I'd sit in my living room with my blanket, tea, and remote, and watch anything that could make me forget for a little while. Kevin Hart. Mo'Nique. Eddie Murphy. Martin reruns. Steve Harvey. The Kings of Comedy.

There were days I'd laugh so hard I'd have to pause the TV because the tears running down my face weren't from sadness — they were from relief.

Laughter became my therapy. It reminded me that life still had joy.

You can't hold fear and laughter at the same time — they don't live in the same space. So, I chose laughter. Every single day.

Healing Through Nourishment

I started taking silver water, iodine, mineral greens, and a liquid complex multivitamin daily, and cut out processed foods and sugar. I began to understand food differently. It wasn't just about eating — it was about fueling my healing.

Even on the hardest days, when people came to check on me, I'd still cook for them. My kitchen became my sanctuary. When I cooked, I felt alive again.

Music, Movement, and Momentum

Some days, the only thing that could shift my energy was music. I'd put on something upbeat — old-school R&B, gospel, or anything that made me feel alive — and I'd dance. Movement became medicine. It wasn't about exercise — it was proof of life.

My Circle of Strength

My tribe wasn't large — it was loyal. My son and my friends were my world during that time. But I also learned to protect my peace. My space was sacred — reserved for healing, humor, and hope.

Gratitude as Medicine

Every night before bed, I made myself list three things I was grateful for. Some nights it was deep: "I'm still here." Other nights, it was simple: "The tea was hot. My son made me laugh."

Closing Reflection

I didn't beat cancer by pretending it wasn't hard. I beat it by living every day like it didn't own me. Once you build your survival toolkit — once you learn how to protect your peace, nourish your body, laugh through your pain, and strengthen your spirit — life can throw anything at you… and you'll just smile and say, "I've got the tools for that."

CHAPTER FOUR

When the storm finally quieted, I didn't know how to feel. For months, my life had been about survival — test results, appointments, treatments, prayers. Every day was a countdown or a climb. Then suddenly, it was quiet.

The doctors said "remission." The calls slowed down. The chaos eased up.

And I remember thinking, What now?

Because nobody tells you that surviving is just the beginning.

The Quiet After the Chaos

I remember waking up one morning to sunlight pouring through the window — no doctors, no IVs, no blood tests — just quiet. For months, my body had been in fight mode. Now that it was calm, I didn't know what to do with it. Then I laughed — I was still here.

Dealing with Cancer in a World That Stopped

Right at the beginning of my diagnosis, COVID-19 hit. Everything stopped. And for a moment, I thought, Lord, I didn't mean it like that! But when the entire planet shut down, I didn't feel so alone anymore. Healing doesn't always happen in motion. Sometimes it happens in stillness.

Relearning How to Live

After fighting for your life, you start to see everything differently. I didn't rush back into the world — I reintroduced myself to it.

My New Relationship with the Mirror

When my hair grew back, it came in silver — bold, undeniable, divine. With my sister cousin Tamika's help, we made it fun to get creative with styles and find my new look. That platinum gray became my superhero cape.

Living in Color Again

As the months passed, I found my rhythm. I worked. I wrote. I dreamed. I loved color again — in my clothes, my food, my energy, my world.

Closing Reflection

Cancer made me stop. COVID made the world stop. But God used both to make me start — healing, feeling, living. And that's my superpower: living on purpose, every day.

CHAPTER FIVE

WHEN YOU WALK THROUGH FIRE

When you walk through fire and come out standing, you don't just go back to life as usual — you walk differently.

The heat changes your stride. The flames refine what remains. You start to move with quiet strength and unshakable peace because you've already seen what tried to destroy you and lived to tell the story.

Survival changes you, but thriving transforms you.

I hadn't just survived cancer. I had survived everything that ever tried to break me — heartbreak, loss, disappointment, exhaustion, and fear. Every wound, every scar, every sleepless night became part of a deeper story: not of what hurt me, but of what healed me.

And I came out not angry at life, but grateful for it.

THE AWAKENING

Before cancer, I was living fast — too fast to notice I was running on empty. My calendar was packed, my inbox overflowing, and my phone rarely silent. From the outside, it looked like success. But inside, my spirit was whispering for rest.

When cancer arrived, it didn't knock — it broke the door down. It forced me to stop. Suddenly, I couldn't hide behind busyness or deadlines. I had to face myself — my fears, my faith, my future.

And for the first time in years, I listened.

The awakening didn't happen overnight. It came slowly, like dawn breaking after a long night.

I realized I had spent years doing instead of being.

I had built a life full of accomplishments but empty of alignment.

Cancer stripped away everything that was shallow. It made me confront what mattered. And when I walked through that fire, I promised myself that if I ever got another chance, I would live differently.

After that, I stopped chasing success. I started chasing significance. I didn't want applause — I wanted peace. I wanted a life that mattered when no one was watching.

LIVING WITH INTENTION

I stopped filling my schedule and started filling my soul.

I began each morning not by checking my messages, but by checking in with myself. I asked, what do I need today? Who do I want to be today?

I learned to say "no" without guilt and "yes" without fear.

"No" became a complete sentence.

"Yes" became sacred.

Boundaries became my love language — not walls to keep people out, but gates that decided who had earned the right to come in.

Peace became a person I protect.

And protecting that peace became an act of daily worship.

I stopped mistaking movement for progress. Some days, rest was the most productive thing I could do. I learned that slowing down doesn't mean giving up — it means showing up differently.

Living with intention isn't about perfection. It's about presence. It's choosing to walk in gratitude even when the road gets rough, to find joy in the simple, and to treat each moment as holy ground.

REDEFINING PURPOSE

As my body healed, my purpose expanded. I started speaking — first quietly, then boldly. I began writing, mentoring, and sharing pieces of my journey with others who were fighting their own battles. The more I shared, the lighter I felt.

My pain had a purpose.

My story became a lifeline.

I realized that purpose isn't found in what you do — it's revealed through what you overcome.

That's when the phrase "purpose-led healing" came to life for me.

It means choosing to see every scar as sacred. It means leading from a place of empathy, not ego. It means allowing your healing to heal others.

I stopped asking, "Why me?" and started asking, "What now?"

That question changed everything.

Because when your pain becomes your platform, your life stops being about survival — it becomes about service.

FAITH AS FOUNDATION

There were days when I didn't know what tomorrow would look like.

Days when the diagnosis felt louder than hope.

Days when I had no choice but to surrender.

When I didn't know what was next, I didn't panic — I prayed.

Faith became my foundation, not my fallback. It grounded me when fear tried to take over. Prayer wasn't a last resort — it was my daily breath.

God didn't always give me answers, but He always gave me peace.

Sometimes faith meant believing without evidence, trusting without clarity, and walking without sight. But every time I did, I found light waiting on the other side of darkness.

Faith taught me that peace isn't the absence of struggle — it's the strength to stand in the middle of it and still say, *"It is well."*

Through every appointment, every uncertainty, every prayer whispered through tears, I felt guided — not just healed but held.

THE BEAUTY IN BECOMING

Before, I wanted to get "back to normal." But one day I realized — normal was the thing that nearly broke me.

I didn't need to go back. I needed to become.

Healing wasn't about returning to who I was before cancer; it was about unveiling who I was meant to be all along.

I was being refined, reshaped, redefined.

The process of becoming isn't pretty. It's messy and uncertain. It's filled with doubt and detours. But somewhere along the way, you start to recognize the beauty in the broken places — the light seeping through the cracks.

I stopped apologizing for outgrowing people and places that no longer aligned with my peace. Growth sometimes looks like goodbye.

Becoming is brave work. It's choosing to live in truth even when comfort calls you back to the old you. It's allowing your evolution to offend those who preferred your silence.

But I wasn't here to please anymore — I was here to be.

LEGACY, NOT LABELS

My favorite titles aren't found on a business card. They live in the lives I've touched: Survivor. Mother. Healer. Human.

I used to chase labels — accomplishments, recognition, approval.

Now I chase legacy.

Legacy isn't about fame or followers. It's about the fingerprints you leave on souls.

It's about the quiet moments — the text that encouraged someone, the conversation that gave someone courage, the story that reminded someone they're not alone.

If my journey can help another person stand taller, love deeper, or believe again — then every trial was worth it.

Legacy is not built in the spotlight. It's built in the shadows of surrender, where purpose and humility meet.

The echo I want my story to leave isn't *"she survived."* It's *"she helped me believe I could too."*

THE RETURN TO JOY

Joy became my compass.

I stopped waiting for perfect moments and started creating them. I celebrated the ordinary — morning light through the window, laughter around the table, a song that reminded me I'm still here.

Each breath became a small hallelujah.

Gratitude became my daily ritual. I wrote it, spoke it, lived it. Gratitude shifted my perspective from what I lost to what I learned.

Joy isn't loud; it's steady. It's the soft hum of peace that stays even when life isn't easy.

I realized that happiness depends on what happens, but joy depends on what you choose. And every day, I chose joy — even in the waiting, even in the wondering.

CLOSING REFLECTION:
BECOMING UNSTOPPABLE

Before cancer, I chased success. After cancer, I chased significance.

And in that chase, I found *myself.*

I learned that survival is about breathing, but thriving is about believing. Believing that life still has purpose. That pain can birth promise. That endings can become awakenings.

I am no longer defined by what I endured. I am defined by what I *became* because of it.

I am no longer afraid of fire — I've learned to walk through it.

I am no longer afraid of storms — I've learned to dance in the rain.

I am no longer just a survivor.

I am the evidence that light always wins.

And that is what makes me unstoppable "PERIOD"!

EPILOGUE: THE UNFINISHED CHAPTER

Healing doesn't have a finish line — it's a lifestyle. Cancer didn't destroy me. It introduced me to myself.

If you're reading this and going through your own storm, remember you don't need to know how you'll make it. Just believe that you will. Your story is still unfolding — beautifully.

AUTHOR'S NOTE

If you've made it to this page, I want to say thank you.

Writing this wasn't easy. There were moments when I had to stop typing because I couldn't see through the tears — and others that brought me right back to hospital rooms and quiet nights where faith was all I had left.

You don't have to be fearless to be faithful. You don't have to have it all together to start healing. You just have to begin.

When life feels heavy, say it with me: "F*** this. I'm living."

— Marli Blackman

AFTERWORD: FOR EVERY SURVIVOR

For every soul who's ever stared into the dark and still reached for the light — this is for you.

You are not your diagnosis. You are the sunrise that refused to stop shining. Some days you'll feel fragile. Some days you'll feel fierce. And some days, you'll be both — and that's still victory.

As long as you're still here, your story isn't over. It's just the next chapter. Unwritten. Unfolding. Unstoppable.

— With all my heart, Marli Blackman

FEEL-GOOD WATCHLIST: LAUGHTER IS MEDICINE

When you've cried enough, when the house is too quiet, when your spirit needs a little lift — press play.

Movies That Made Me Laugh Out Loud

1. Coming to America (1988)
2. The Nutty Professor
3. Friday
4. Girls Trip
5. Barbershop
6. Bridesmaids
7. Harlem Nights
8. The Best Man Holiday
9. Think Like a Man
10. This Christmas

Stand-Up Specials That Gave Me Life

1. Kevin Hart — "Laugh at My Pain"
2. Wanda Sykes — "Not Normal"
3. Dave Chappelle — "Sticks & Stones"
4. Earthquake — "Legendary"
5. Mo'Nique — "I Coulda Been Your Cellmate"
6. Cedric the Entertainer — "Live from the V lle"
7. Martin Lawrence — "You So Crazy"
8. Katt Williams — "The Pimp Chronicles Pt. 1"
9. Ali Wong — "Baby Cobra"
10. Eddie Murphy — "Delirious"

Prescription: Watch one. Laugh hard. Repeat daily.

HEALING WORD SEARCH:

"WHEN I'M BETTER..."

```
Y L A U G H T E R A U P X L J
S R L I V E R D F Y G Y L Q L
C R H C G J A A A V I R V M L
N K E P Z D V N Z T X Q O L D
P B N S H I E C F C O O K W B
R U F H T S L E T V X B P P E
C S R A S T R E N G T H W K M
T R K P I I K S Q W U E S A V
S I N G O T P W W R I T E X K
Q E T P M S H I N Q P E A C E
P W N X S Y E R E B U I L D U
R B Y J H S C M F H Y F Q F L
A D J S O E Z B M M Y L O V E
Y X Z R S Y A L F G L O W C J
S V M X J X B L S M I L E V D
```

Word List: LAUGHTER · FAITH · PEACE · STRENGTH · PURPOSE · TRAVEL · COOK · DANCE · HEAL · WRITE · PRAY · SING · REST · GLOW · LOVE · SMILE · GROW · LIVE · ENJOY · REBUILD

First thing I'm doing when I'm better.

JOY JOURNAL PROMPTS

Daily Gratitude

1. Today, I'm grateful for…

2. A small moment that made me smile was…

3. Someone who showed me kindness today was…

4. The sound that made me feel peaceful was…

5. Right now, I feel closest to God when…

Healing Reflections

1. What lesson did my hardest day teach me?

2. Who or what helped me find laughter again?

3. What does "being alive" feel like to me now?

4. What part of myself am I most proud of today?

5. What does peace look like for me?

Joy & Laughter

1. Three things that make me laugh no matter what are…

2. A song that always lifts my spirit is…

3. My comfort movie or show is…

4. If joy had a color, it would be…

5. The funniest moment I've had since healing was…

Looking Forward

1. Something I want to try for the first time is…

2. A place I want to visit when I'm ready is…

3. One way I can bring more laughter into my days is…

4. One promise I'm making to myself is…

5. I am becoming the woman who…

ACKNOWLEDGMENTS

To God — my healer, my anchor, my everything. Thank You for the grace that carried me, for the lessons that reshaped me, and for the peace that rebuilt me from the inside out.

To my sons, Frank Jr. and Arrington (RIP) — you are my forever why.

Frank, you made motherhood a piece of cake; you are the best human I know.

Arrington, my sweet bonus baby — your spirit walks beside us every day. You took care of your little brother while he checked on me. I love you beyond heaven and earth.

To my family and tribe — Malika, Ardra, Tamika, Toya, Essence, Eric, Mama and Papa Hunter, Aunt Charlotte, and all my girls who held me up when I couldn't stand — thank you for your prayers, your patience, and your laughter.

To Malika — you took on cancer with me. You walked it out to the end. You show up and show out for me every single time. I love you deeply.

To my ex-husband, Frank — thank you for supporting our son during one of the toughest times of his life. Thank you for taking me to surgery because our son insisted on being there, and I didn't want him to be alone waiting for the doctors. Your presence meant more than words.

To my sister-in-law "Cindy" — girl, you are just the absolute best. You always understand the assignment when it comes to our boys. You show up and show out, always. I can't say enough about you. I love you.

A special thank you to my girl **T-White**, aka **Tasha Mack**, for encouraging me to get this book written as fast as I have — thank you, girl.

Ardra — I will spend my days loving and appreciating your love and dedication to me. I couldn't have gotten through that without you.

Cheron — you had just gone through the fire, only to have to support your girl the very next year. For that, we have a bond that is unbreakable.

To my childhood BFF **Gina** — you would give me your right arm if I asked. I love you with all my heart.

If I've missed your name, know this: I love you. Cancer brain is real, and sometimes the fog is thick — but my love and gratitude for you are crystal clear.

To my doctors and healers — thank you for your care, compassion, and belief in me. You are part of my miracle.

And to every reader holding this book — thank you for letting me share my story with you. If it gave you even one ounce of hope, peace, or laughter, then my mission is complete.

With endless gratitude, love, and faith,

— Marli Blackman